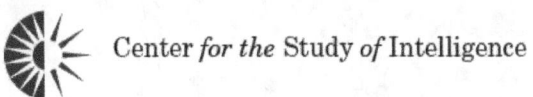 Center *for the* Study *of* Intelligence

Center *for the* Study *of* Intelligence
Roundtable Report

Intelligence and Policy:

The Evolving Relationship

10 November 2003
Georgetown University,
Washington, D.C.

Washington, D.C.
June 2004

Central Intelligence Agency

Introduction

As became abundantly clear during a conference sponsored by CIA's Center for the Study of Intelligence (CSI) in Charlottesville, Virginia, on 10 and 11 September 2003, the challenges that face the US Intelligence Community in the aftermath of the terrorist attack on the United States two years earlier are perceived by members of that community as being far more complex, demanding, and consequential than any they have heretofore encountered. That conference brought together an experienced group of national security specialists from the intelligence and policy communities to discuss *Intelligence for a New Era in American Foreign Policy*.

Not long after the Charlottesville conference, Dr. James Steiner, CIA's Officer in Residence and Associate at the Institute for the Study of Diplomacy (ISD) of the Edmund A. Walsh School of Foreign Service at Georgetown University, coordinated an effort to answer one of the challenging questions that have arisen in the changed post-9/11 security environment: how can the Intelligence Community effectively provide "actionable" intelligence while being mindful of its traditional practice of separating, to the extent possible, the intelligence and policy functions of national security decisionmaking. The resulting one-day roundtable conference became for CSI the first in a planned series of projects on intelligence and policy intended to foster better understanding of the often-perplexing dynamic between the consumers of intelligence and intelligence professionals.

The roundtable, *Where Is the Red Line? Actionable Intelligence vs. Policy Advocacy*, took place on 10 November 2003 at Georgetown University. Instead of using a conference format, with formal papers and designated commentators, the roundtable was conducted as a discussion among a relatively small circle of participants, divided about equally between professional (current or former) intelligence officers and senior intelligence consumers drawn from the ranks of former policymakers. Ambassador Thomas Pickering, former Under Secretary of State for Political Affairs, and a former Deputy Director of Central Intelligence, Richard Kerr, served as cochairmen.

In addition to the cochairmen, participants included:

- Frans Bax, President, CIA University

- Hans Binnendijk, Director, Center for Technology and National Security Policy, National Defense University; Special Assistant to the President and Senior Director for Defense Policy and Arms Control, National Security Council, 1999–2001

- Dennis Blair, Admiral, USN (ret.); President, Institute for Defense Analyses; former Commander-in-Chief, Pacific Command; former Assistant Director of Central Intelligence for Military Support

- Christopher Bolan, Colonel, US Army; ISD Associate; former member of the staffs of vice presidents Gore and Cheney, focusing on Middle East issues

- Chester Crocker, James R. Schlesinger Professor of Strategic Studies, Edmund A. Walsh School of Foreign Service, Georgetown University; Chairman, US Institute of Peace; Assistant Secretary of State for African Affairs, 1981–89

- James Dobbins, Director, International Security and Defense Policy Center, RAND Corporation; served in a variety of State Department and White House posts, including Assistant Secretary of State for European Affairs and Ambassador to the European Union; also served as US special envoy for Afghanistan, for Kosovo, for Bosnia, for Haiti, and for Somalia

- Carl Ford, Assistant Secretary of State for Intelligence and Research, 2001–2003; Principal Deputy Assistant Secretary of Defense for International Security Affairs, 1989–93

- Paul Johnson, Director, Center for the Study of Intelligence

- Woodrow Kuhns, Deputy Director, Center for the Study of Intelligence

- Douglas MacEachin, staff member, National Commission on Terrorist Attacks Upon the United States (9/11 Commission); Deputy Director for Intelligence, CIA, 1993–95; Senior Research Fellow, John F. Kennedy School of Government, Harvard University, 1995–2000

- John MacGaffin, former Senior Adviser to the Director and Deputy Director, Federal Bureau of Investigation; former Associate Deputy Director for Operations, CIA

- William Nolte, Deputy Assistant Director of Central Intelligence for Analysis and Production

- Phyllis Oakley, Chair of the Board, US Committee for the United Nations Population Fund; Assistant Secretary of State for Intelligence and Research, 1997–98; and Assistant Secretary of State for Population, Refugees, and Migration, 1994–97

- Martin Petersen, Deputy Executive Director, CIA

- Jennifer Sims, Visiting Professor, Edmund A. Walsh School of Foreign Service, Georgetown University; Deputy Assistant Secretary of State for Intelligence Coordination, 1994–98; Intelligence Adviser to the Under Secretary of State for Management and Coordinator for Intelligence Resources and Planning, 1998–2001

- James Steiner, CIA Officer-in-Residence, ISD

• Casimir Yost, Marshall Coyne Professor in the Practice of Diplomacy, Edmund A. Walsh School of Foreign Service, Georgetown University; Director, ISD

The following summary of roundtable proceedings does not attempt to recapitulate the discussions in detail. It attempts, rather, to focus on the most salient points made by the participants as they considered a set of key questions drawn up in advance by the roundtable sponsors. These questions will be found at the conclusion of the text. Readers will note that some of the questions were discussed more extensively than others.

Those interested in sampling the tenor of the discussions may refer to the italicized excerpts contained in each section.

Contents

The Policy Community-Intelligence Community Nexus

In a sense, you could start off by making the assumption that it is inevitable that, if the machinery works well, intelligence shapes policy.

The Intelligence Community Views Its Customers

The observation of a former senior intelligence officer that, in his experience, intelligence analysts often knew more about the countries they followed than they did about the customers they served led roundtable participants initially to debate the nature of the target audience for Intelligence Community products. One rather expansive definition held that anyone on the receiving end of an intelligence product could conceivably make policy, including, for example, a member of the armed forces in the field who chose to take action on the basis of a tactical intelligence report. Such a recipient, it was suggested, might, however, more aptly be considered a policy "implementer" than a policy "maker."

Pursuing this line, a roundtable participant thought that "decisionmaker" might be a more useful definition in that a customer could well be a "policymaker" at one point and a "policy implementer" at another point. Moreover, the speaker suggested, as an intelligence consumer moved along this spectrum, the nature of his dialogue with analysts would change, as would the products they provided in response.

Other participants preferred a more restrictive definition that excluded tactical-level consumers and focused on consumers at the policy level. These consumers would certainly include the president, the cabinet, the cabinet deputies, and those holding assistant secretary-level positions in the various departments. Speakers then suggested that key consumers might also include officials given special, high-level assignments; key cabinet and congressional staff members; and those heading delegations to important negotiations.

A former senior intelligence officer cautioned against trying to arrive at too precise a definition of a policymaker, arguing that identifying the audience and matching product and audience are part of the intelligence professional's job. Further to that observation, a speaker noted that the number of officials who see themselves as having a role to play in the policy process has increased, as has the number of agencies they represent, both of which increase the demands levied on the resources available to the Intelligence Community.

Discussion Excerpts

By intelligence, you could mean one of two things: you could mean information obtained clandestinely, or you could mean any product of the Intelligence Community. I assume you mean the latter, since a lot of the Intelligence Community products are derived from overtly obtained material.

* * *

Some intelligence providers are also players— verification has been one, covert action is another. Any intelligence operation overseas has some policy significance.

* * *

When you add covert action to the mix and try to figure out who is the policy implementer or not . . . is the CIA officer in the field with Masood an implementer or a collector? The answer is: "Yes."

* * *

This notion that policymakers can do intelligence as well as the Intelligence Community is flat bullshit. There's too much information. The volume is so great that any policymaker who believes that he can look at that and come up with good answers is a fool. And you ought not to provide them with intelligence anyway. But the problem is that the Intelligence Community hasn't recognized that as well. Shame on us if we can't do better

. . . I would be much happier with competent policymakers who know a lot about the subject they're dealing with, but know enough to know that they won't ever know as much as a really good intelligence analyst.

than policymakers. We can get more information out of what we're collecting; we're just not doing it.

* * *

In the last two administrations I had experience with, we spent a lot of our time trying to figure out how the people coming in functioned— what their biases and their interests were. I mean, we spent a lot of time on intelligence focused on the principal players, and it was worth every minute of it.

What Policymakers Want From Intelligence

Roundtable participants recognized that policymakers desire both substantive and bureaucratic support from the Intelligence Community. On the substantive side, they want reliable information on new developments and on matters with which they are unfamiliar. They also want intelligence to inform their decisionmaking by describing the choices available to an adversary or an opposing negotiator and explaining how and why one choice or another might be preferred. On the bureaucratic side, they want intelligence to give them an edge in policy deliberations. Several speakers spoke admiringly of senior policymakers who developed a close relationship with their opposite numbers in intelligence in order to give themselves an advantage over bureaucratic rivals.

Participants with an intelligence background observed that the policymakers they have served have had quite different approaches to the Intelligence Community and different styles in dealing with their analytical interlocutors. For example, some have begun by professing little use for intelligence and much confidence in their own knowledge and ability to make policy decisions. Others have appeared awestruck by the intelligence products they were offered.

These contrasting attitudes, it was noted, have generally reached a "crossover" point at which a rough balance in approaches was achieved.

A speaker with experience in both policy and intelligence positions commented that most policymakers failed to make efficient use of the capabilities of the Intelligence Community, relying on analysts to think up the questions they should want answered. Other participants added a caveat, however. In their view, even when policymakers actively solicit input from the Intelligence Community, intelligence officers must be wary of responding to the questions in their own terms. These participants argued that, if necessary, analysts should recast the questions to make sure that their analyses are not compromised by a partisan agenda and that the issues that should be addressed *are* addressed.

Several participants raised the question of bias and its role in causing intelligence failures. The discussion focused on several aspects. On the one hand, intelligence producers can be responsible for failures through erroneous assumptions or personal prejudice. Consumers, on the other hand, often cause failures through reluctance to accept intelligence they don't want to hear.

Continuing on this theme, participants recognized the practically limitless volume of information, both classified and unclassified, that is now available to policymakers. This, they added, has led many policymakers to conclude that they can do their own analysis. Several speakers noted that, although many policymakers could point to some prior foreign policy experience, this approach could be harmful because it prevents the policymaker from taking advantage of the knowledge that years of study affords analysts.

There was agreement among participants that, despite its expense and inefficiency, having more than one intelligence agency competing for the consumer's attention has generally served the country well. Several speakers added that they would not be troubled by additional competition—one example being *boutiques* created for a specific purpose by individual policymakers—so long as all producers were subject to the same rules. A former policymaker pointed out that the US model of an intelligence system differed from those of several key allies, which are either more restrictive or more freewheeling.

The same former policymaker reminded participants of the commonly held view that intelligence analysts almost always tend toward pessimism in their appraisals because they are more likely to be criticized for failing to predict an untoward event than for making a call that turns out to be wrong. Policymakers, on the other hand, tend to be optimists. Occasionally, however, when they are reluctant to take action on some issue, policymakers are happy to receive a pessimistic assessment. Such conjunctures, he noted, work against policy change and discourage innovative thinking.

A speaker commented on the difficulty analysts encounter in gaining acceptance for scenarios with non-linear outcomes. This prompted another participant to lament that war gaming, which sometimes produced such results by bringing analysts and policymakers together in structured exercises, had fallen into disuse in recent years.

Discussion Excerpts

But one of the things I observed is that some administrations came in saying, "Intelligence can't help me at all. I don't like it. I don't trust it. I am not confident in it. I have my own way of thinking about problems, thank you very much. We'll take your stuff, but don't expect a great deal of interaction." Another group came in saying, "This is an omnipotent group… [it] knows everything. I can hardly wait to embrace 'em." All of them changed their views.

The ones that were skeptical when they came in became increasingly dependent or, at least, reliant on it. The ones that loved it at the beginning began to say, "Is that all you can do for me?" So you cross somewhere in the center . . . .

* * *

The goals of a player in a bureaucratic warfare game are, first, control. Second, power. And power comes from expertise; so you need intelligence to win battles that are about expertise, and you need intelligence to be able to be effective with the foreigner as well. Thirdly, to achieve your goals, whatever those goals might be, to exploit those opportunities, to carry out that policy. And fourth on my list is to support the national interest. These are in descending order.

* * *

In the policy formulation process, people can act very tactically as they're trying to grab a role in doing policy. Policymakers, on any given issue, aren't necessarily a static set. They are competing to get into the policy domain, and they want intelligence to support them in the tactical process of getting an "in" on an issue.

* * *

Quite often, policymakers do not want intelligence on a problem they do not want to hear; or they've already heard the answer, and they don't like it.

* * *

Policymakers, fundamentally, are doers, particularly early in an administration. They tend to have strong personalities. They come in with an agenda, and, often, they think they come in with a mandate. And, therefore, I think what they are looking for from intelligence, particularly early on, is information that helps them push that agenda.

* * *

I think the intelligence suppliers have to understand that policymakers have an agenda. They have both a bureaucratic one, and they have, perhaps, a substantive agenda. Bureaucratically, they're trying to enhance their own position in a kind of zero-sum game vis-à-vis everyone else in the same sphere. Substantively, they probably have a set of objectives they're committed to trying to achieve. And that means that they will respond to some kinds of intelligence differently than others—that they will respond better to intelligence that enhances either their position or their chances of achieving their substantive objective and that they will at least regard more skeptically intelligence which has the opposite effect.

* * *

Probably you'll go back and find most intelligence failures are not because of lack of information, but because of assumptions and predictions that were based on biases.

* * *

A colleague once used weather forecasting as opposed to predicting: "I've got high pressure, so much temperature. If nothing changes, and if my assumption about this is correct, this is where the thing's going to come out." But, if I sit down and say, "This is how they think, this is what they'll do, and, therefore, this is the outcome"—that's the recipe for disaster.

* * *

But the terms of reference [of a National Intelligence Estimate] were defined not by the Agency, but by the requester . . . in my view a very dangerous process, and a thing that had

been resisted, at least in my experience, for as long as I could remember. And that is, when the Hill asked for an estimate, or the policymaker asked for an estimate, that's fine. But recast the terms of the estimate in terms that you wish to address.

* * *

When someone sits at a desk at the NSC and sees all of the raw take, does that mean that that policymaker doesn't have to rely on the Intelligence Community as much as he or she would have a decade ago or two decades ago, and does that make it easier for the policymaker to say, "I don't need the intel community; I'm going to have my own analysts sitting here taking a look at this and reaching our own conclusions, and, therefore, I can cut out the intel community?"

* * *

If somebody wants to create his own little intelligence cell, fine. But, subject it to the same competition that the rest of us have to go through. But what the problem is, organizations are created. They're not subjected to the kinds of competition and transparency [as the rest of us].

* * *

By and large, my experience is that almost all the analytical agencies have the same stuff, and, so, then I think what good decisionmakers value is our different opinions. I mean, the best part of NIEs used to be the footnotes.

* * *

There's an interesting distinction between the American intelligence system and the British intelligence system . . . and the German. The American, in principle, is open and competitive. That is, everybody has access to all the information. Each of the agencies can come to its own conclusions. They are not forced to a common conclusion, and they can brief those conclusions to anybody they want. The British system is open, but coordinated. That is, intelligence agencies aren't permitted to brief their conclusions to policymakers except through the Joint Intelligence Committee, which is chaired by a policymaker and which comes to a coordinated judgment, and only that coordinated judgment goes to the policymakers. And [there's] the German system, which is neither transparent nor coordinated; in which the intelligence agencies secretly pass such information as they choose to such policymakers as they wish.

* * *

But one of the things that, it seemed to me, rescued us a number of times was a deep, deep understanding of the facts and the issues at a level of detail where you could go into a room and defend your argument. I do have the impression right now that we go into rooms unarmed to deal with serious critics who know a lot.

* * *

I think policymakers and decisionmakers can fancy that they are, in fact, better than the intelligence analysts because they get the same data. The only thing they don't have is 30 years' worth of looking at this country and what that does in the brain cells in the back of the brain, which it doesn't if you've been doing other things for 30 years.

But one of the things that . . . rescued us a number of times was a deep, deep understanding of the facts and the issues at a level of detail where you could go into a room and defend your argument.

The Evolving Role of the Intelligence Community

Keeping Up with the Competition

Participants recognized that there has been a marked change in the role of intelligence since the end of the Cold War. Until the 1990s, the Intelligence Community virtually "owned" information on the USSR and the communist world, the principal strategic challenge facing the United States and its allies, because most of that information was acquired clandestinely or technically. Developments of the past 15 years have vastly increased the amount of information available to policymakers, however, and have deprived the Intelligence Community of its dominant position. A speaker added that the volume of available information is growing steadily as a result of the current emphasis on collection.

Several participants saw problems in the increasing focus of intelligence producers on current intelligence and policy support at the expense of basic research. In their view, while the Intelligence Community does a good job of providing policymakers with current intelligence, this shift in emphasis has produced a lack of analytic depth that all too often makes intelligence products little or no better than what most reasonably sophisticated policymakers can provide for themselves. The problem is made more acute in that a large percentage of the intelligence workforce is relatively new on the job.

Other speakers, arguing that policymakers perforce focus on events of the moment and are able to peruse only a relatively small amount of the information available to them, advocated efforts by analysts to take advantage of their ability to concentrate on a richer store of information to look for ways to give policymakers products that provide needed context for the intelligence reports that cross their desks. Carrying the argument a step further, another speaker commented on the importance of analysts' having sufficient knowledge of their fields, as well as an understanding of the way in which policies are developed, so as to be able to give policymakers intelligence analyses they may not even realize they need.

Another participant, a former high-level intelligence officer, contended that the Intelligence Community's efforts to maintain analytical relevance should include a requirement for systematic critiques of Community products. In addition, the inclusion of policymakers in such critiques would make it more likely that the needs of the policy community were taken into account. This observation provided a counterpoint to an earlier suggestion that, to the extent possible, policymakers should include intelligence officers in their meetings, so that policy community concerns and needs might be conveyed to their colleagues more accurately and expeditiously.

Discussion Excerpts

I think there is a fundamental change in the role of intelligence since the end of the Cold War, where intelligence provided the bulk of the knowledge and information on the strategic problem. And it was secret. It was clandestinely acquired, or technically acquired, and, therefore, intelligence essentially owned that information. Today, there is no ownership of information by the Intelligence Community.

* * *

The Intelligence Community really [is] focused on current intelligence, on policy support. It does very little research. It has very little understanding below the level of the policymaker and, in my view, on many issues. I think that, in some ways, these two groups are reinforcing each other's worst habits.

* * *

If you focus on current intelligence, that's about ten percent of the information available to the Intelligence Community. The Intelligence Community is really the only one in town that has the time to look at the other 90 percent and find the things that don't stick out to the current intelligence officer or the policymaker the first time around. In fact, my observation is that policymakers often know more than the intelligence officers, particularly the senior ones, because they've been on the telephone to the King of Tut or to the president of Wa. And they talk to people all the time. They talk to the President; they know what the Secretary of State and the Secretary of Defense know, and intelligence officers don't have any real access to that sort of knowledge. The fact is that most policymakers are starving for new knowledge. And if it's good, if it's new, I don't care how skeptical they are, you can sell it to them.

* * *

Your average analyst today, and certainly one working terrorism, is probably seeing in the tenths of what's available. Furthermore, we're pouring so much money into collection systems and very little into the exploitation of that collection, that the problem is getting bigger. We've got to put more money into the analytic side and balance the collection, or we're just going to be another opinion.

* * *

The sheer volume of information, the sheer growth of consumers, the pressure to do it quickly, has driven research out of the market.

Challenges for Analysts

The discussion of how the analytical community should most effectively package and deliver its product to the policy community led to an exchange on the content of those products. There was ready agreement that one of the major developments since the terrorist

attacks of September 2001 is that the standard for analytic success has changed dramatically from that of the Cold War, when the question of whether or not intelligence was performing well against the Soviet target lacked practical relevance for most Americans. Now, on the other hand, in the war against terrorism, public expectations of intelligence have become unreasonably high—as one speaker put it, "like expecting the FBI to stop bank robberies before they occur."

Not surprisingly, there was also general agreement that analysts must strive to avoid both strict reportage and outright advocacy of personal points-of-view. Drawing on his extensive experience supporting US delegations, one speaker argued that analytic advocacy had to be distinguished from analytic advice, in which the service that intelligence performs is to describe alternatives and their potential consequences, including those that point out flaws in positions policymakers favored and those that present the least bad of a series of bad choices. Another speaker cautioned that analysts should not dwell on personal perceptions of the correctness or incorrectness of policy decisions, noting that such fixations occasionally cause higher-ups to "jerk" the system in order to redirect its focus toward the current situation and its actual alternatives. (He added that some might find that such a directed shift in emphasis constitutes "politicization.")

Further to this discussion, participants commented on the contrast between military practice—where subordinates are expected to argue their points-of-view vigorously until a decision is made, after which they are expected to give full support to that decision— and that of intelligence, where the fact that a policy decision has been made does not require analysts to cut their analyses to that cloth. It was noted that their insistence on "speaking truth to power"—mentioned by a number of observers as a long-time Directorate of Intelligence cultural trait—has frequently caused analysts to be regarded as less than welcome guests at the tables where policy is debated.

Several participants wondered if this culture of speaking forthrightly extended to internal Agency deliberations on such matters, for example, as covert action. In response, several speakers argued that an independent stance was not only possible but a necessary aspect of analytic "checks and balances," even if the critiquing process led to in-house clashes. A former senior intelligence officer reminded participants that the failed Bay of Pigs operation of 1961 had been one from which the analytic side of the house had been completely excluded.

Discussion Excerpts

A former senior intelligence officer: *It's seldom that the Intelligence [Community] looks for policy opportunity. I mean, looks at the good side. I mean, it doesn't say, "Boy, here's something that's really interesting that you could do."*

A former senior policymaker: *Well, that's not your day or night job yet. It's somebody else's.*

* * *

I think where we want to be is in that middle ground between the Sherman Kent school, which basically dominated the estimative process up until 1973, and where we've come since then. Sherman Kent's view was that it was important for the estimative process pretty much to be detached from policy and to be highly objective. So, [by] making sure that the intelligence community had an ivory tower to do that basic research, you would be providing something the policymaker couldn't get in his busy day. But the downfall of that was that what estimates were produced weren't relevant enough from the view of the policymaker, so we went in another direction. And I think it

sounds like what we're saying is that we need to find that middle ground and perhaps get back into the system more of the strategic, long-term, basic research that Sherman Kent advocated for so many years.

* * *

I have yet to find the question that a policymaker would like answered that one analyst can answer. Either it's too general, or it's too detailed. We need to rethink the way we put our analysts together, so that they can better respond to the information and the questions they are receiving.

* * *

But there's a difference, which is that the Intelligence Community is supposed to continue to criticize after the decision has been made, which is more difficult to do. [That] puts them in a very different position from the military. They're not supposed to salute and say, "Yes, sir." They're supposed to tell him he doesn't have any clothes on every day.

* * *

Part of our job is to tell the emperor he has no clothes. But, once the emperor's in the stew pot, you're not doing him any good saying over and over again, "You've got no clothes." . . . Start thinking about what we need to be paying attention to [in order] to achieve whatever the goal was at the end of the day. And if you're an intelligence analyst and you can't get off the issue of whether this is a good or bad decision, it's really, really tough. At that point, senior officials in the Agency have to kind of jerk the whole system and get them to focus on the other thing. And then, what does that look like to the analyst down below? That's politicization.

* * *

We need to rethink the way we put our analysts together, so that they can better respond to the information and the questions they are receiving.

Once the emperor's in the stew pot, you're not doing him any good saying over and over again, "You've got no clothes."

There's been no fundamental change in the DI personality. This contrariness is still there, and, I think, it's something we encourage. It does come down more to core values. And you do hear in the Kent School and CIA University the imperative of speaking truth to power . . . .

* * *

I have found, at least, that the counter often, in the covert area, was the DDI's willingness to strike an independent stance, independent of the covert action, and assess it. . . . If you want to have real problems, send the covert action people off by themselves. We've had that, you know. We had the Bay of Pigs, where there was no DI involvement.

* * *

We're putting analysts much closer to operators, both on covert action and operations in an effort to get smarter operations and smarter covert action . . . . The risk, of course, is that you begin to blur these lines. And are you somehow co-opting the analytic function? One reason why we've succeeded . . . in not doing that is we've maintained the analytic units separate from those units with analysts in them that are doing the support to operations, support to covert action.

Challenges for the DCI

Presidents Clinton and Bush charged DCI Tenet with carrying out an active and visible role within the framework of the Middle East peace process and the war on terror. Roundtable participants were divided as to the advisability of DCIs assuming this kind of responsibility. Among the reservations expressed were that such involvement took valuable time from the DCI's statutory duties as manager of the Intelligence Community and that it created the risk that the Intelligence Community's objectivity on that issue would be—or might appear to be—compromised.

In another area touching on DCI responsibilities, there was an extended discussion as to whether there were new realities in the post-9/11 world that might necessitate a reordering of responsibilities within the Intelligence Community. Should the FBI, for example, be divided into an entity with domestic counterintelligence responsibilities and another dedicated to its traditional law enforcement function? This question, although hardly new, has become more salient during the past several years because distinctions between foreign and domestic intelligence have become increasingly blurred and previous conflicts among agencies, particularly the FBI and the CIA, over the uses of intelligence have become better known.

While recognizing the need to address these problems, several participants expressed concern that attempted institutional fixes for Intelligence Community problems, such as reorganizations or creating new agencies, would simply further complicate an already complex picture and permit new, probably unforeseen, dangers to arise. One speaker mentioned that there had been renewed discussion on the advisability of creating the position of Director of National Intelligence with genuine authority over all the Community agencies and the entire Community budget, but several other panelists argued the risks to analytic objectivity and diversity of opinion if a central authority were established.

Roundtable participants agreed that the likelihood of another terrorist attack within the United States was substantial, especially during the run-up to the national election in November 2004. Several foresaw that, in that event, the Intelligence Community might become an easy target of political partisans looking for a scapegoat. This would be all the more likely if a case could be made that a successful attack had been the result of an Intelligence Community failure to correct defects that had been pointed out earlier. The only way to prevent such scapegoating, they agreed, would be for a senior administration official to make clear to the Congress and the public that there are limits to what the Intelligence Community can do to foil terrorist attacks.

Continuing the discussion of a possible second foreign terrorist attack on the United States, a participant commented that the Patriot Act had improved the chances of heading off an attempt but expressed concern that the new authorities granted by the act might tend to infringe on civil liberties. A speaker suggested that not enough had yet been done by federal intelligence and law enforcement agencies to support "first providers" throughout the country. Another participant commented that this could become one of the responsibilities of the new Terrorism Threat Information Center (TTIC) but that questions still remained as to whether the center would focus on analysis or dissemination.

Discussion Excerpts

If the Director of Central Intelligence is responsible for implementing some aspect of the policy, whether he's implementing it overtly or covertly doesn't really make too much difference; he becomes almost axiomatically a proponent of the policy he's implementing . . . . Assuming he does believe in what he's doing, it becomes much less likely that the Intelligence Community will provide a unified product saying that whatever we're doing is a bad idea . . . . You just have to accept that, and it's a question of educating the consumers about what to expect from a bureaucratic arrangement that has those elements to it. This gets to a broader question, which is, is the Intelligence Community supposed to be supporting policy, or is it essentially an adversarial function in which it is supposed to be finding weaknesses and vulnerabilities?

* * *

I'd like us to clarify if the Agency was looking for covert action jobs to do. I would say that they showed about the same degree of enthusiasm as the Joint Chiefs did for any military action, certainly in the last four years of the Clinton administration when I was directly involved. And you probably know that the Chiefs' answer to any military proposal from the State Department was, "Four divisions, four hundred days, four hundred billion dollars."

* * *

What we've got now is the pressure to be perfect, and what we've got in the Patriot Act [are] some tools that allow us to up our chances of performing against that standard. But there's a trade-off, and . . . to the degree that you move it [sic] in one direction, you improve your chances of preventing another 9/11 . . . at the risk of personal liberties and privacy and potential for abuse. You move it [sic] in the other direction you improve those guarantees, but you open yourself here.

* * *

I think that, looking for institutional fixes, one has to be rather careful and recognize that, in fixing one problem, you're going to create another problem. In other words, by shifting organizational boundaries, you'll better handle this issue, but you'll create other things that'll fall between cracks that previously were quite well handled, because you've simply moved those boundaries. But there are always going to be boundaries. If the problem that you're addressing is sufficiently consequential, then it probably does make sense. So, if you're trying to prevent another 9/11-type catastrophe, then creating a Department of Homeland Security . . . is a defensible response, even though it creates a lot of other lacunae in which problems will develop, because there's no longer somebody who's focusing most of his attention on taking care of those problems. And, similarly, I'm sufficiently persuaded by the logic of it to suggest that you need a domestic intelligence agency if your object is to prevent attacks, not prosecute the perpetrators. If your priority attention is to that, the tension between the two functions is sufficient to argue that the two shouldn't be in the same agency.

* * *

One of the things it seems to me is likely to happen out of all this is a strengthening of the DCI authorities and perhaps a movement toward . . . trying the DNI [Director of National Intelligence] kind of theory. Well, one of the serious questions is whether that addresses in any fundamental way the real problems that we've been describing. It's not obvious to me that it does.

* * *

One of the notions behind TTIC was to be a sort of a mechanism to get information at the national level down to first responders . . . . And there's a real debate within our own house over what the nature of that commission really is at the end of the day: whether it's basically an integrator and disseminator of information or whether it's an originator of original source things. It used to be that what was really important was providing and serving the president. Now it's clear that a great deal of what the mission is is the dissemination of actionable intelligence, not just to the Pentagon, but down to the guy who's making the traffic stop in Winslow, Arizona. And we're not trained, we're not equipped, we're not in hand for that mission.

* * *

We are now subject to terrorist attacks that are designed to disrupt and manipulate our internal political process. I believe there is a real risk that terrorist groups will try to exploit

our election season . . . . This is something we've never faced before—an external non-state actor or set of actors trying to influence our political processes.

* * *

I'm still convinced that the biggest set of potential failures doesn't have to do with overlap; it has to do with underlap, that is, failures to meet the exigencies and demands of the intelligence requirements for the policy process and, quite simply, on the other side, failure to meet the exigencies and demands of what's the best selection of policy options in the national interest, broadly looked at, which is constantly, obviously, under stress. At the presidential level, its reelection on the one hand and, secondly, coming up with a policy that serves the national interest but also that doesn't hurt in being reelected . . . .

* * *

I would agree with you that the expectation has changed since 9/11. And somehow we have built up this myth that we know we have the best intelligence in the world, but that we can't know everything. And I think at some point there is going to have to be some sort of, well, probably not a speech, but something to talk to the American public, maybe in the political process, about what intelligence can do and what it can't do, to this point of leveling with the American public.

The Elusive Red Line

During the discussion of the more active and public role assigned to DCI Tenet by Presidents Clinton and Bush, a participant asked if, as a practical matter, this new tasking meant that DCIs are no longer subject to the "red line," the customary demarcation between the intelligence and policy functions. Although opinion on this issue was divided, no participant took the position that these new responsibilities were necessarily inappropriate. In fact, there was general agreement that the idea of a red line is somewhat artificial, especially in the new circumstances since 9/11, and that efforts to impose rigid rules on the intelligence-policy dialogue are likely to prove frustrating.

One roundtable participant favored a flexible approach that recognized that the active involvement of intelligence in a "good" policy initiative would improve the results. (Left unsaid was the obverse of this proposition: that the results of a "bad" policy would presumably be worsened by intelligence involvement.) Another participant commented that he found recently documented derelictions of both policymakers and intelligence organizations and their mutual failures to communicate far more troubling than transgressions of a red line that, for him, was difficult to define. A third speaker saw a loss of competition and transparency as more dangerous for the Intelligence Community than red line issues.

One participant with both policy and intelligence experience provided an example of a kind of "reverse" red line. While he had no objection to policymakers' "intelligent questioning" of analytic judgments, he strongly criticized efforts by policymakers to "bowl over" analysts by using data selectively.

Roundtable participants inclined more toward approaching red line issues as a matter both of principles and of checks and balances. With respect to the former, for example, several participants noted that assisting a policymaker to realize a policy objective might well also promote the political objectives of the

policymaker or his political party. A strict interpretation of the red line concept might preclude such assistance, the speakers noted, but they insisted that taking this political reality into account did not necessarily mean that an intelligence officer's judgments would be compromised. With respect to checks and balances, participants developed a substantial list of actors (including Congress, the media, the public, and academics) and institutional factors (such as organizational structures and internal bureaucratic disputes) that serve most of the time to force policy and intelligence to hew to their accepted roles.

The discussion led to a consensus that the Intelligence Community must recognize the risk of staying close to the policy community but that the potential gains from keeping them in proximity provide ample justification for doing so. In the end, because of the ambiguities they had identified during the day, roundtable participants preferred to see the red line as a more neutral shade, such as gray, and as a line *within* the intelligence-policy relationship and not *between* the two.

Discussion Excerpts

That, at least, raises for me the question of whether there is a red line if it comes to the DCI, or whether we're talking about exceptions at the top and, then, everyone else has to work according to certain rules.

* * *

I think that intelligence officers too easily want to blame the policymaker for their problems. I'm not saying the policymaking process is even logical, let alone perfect, but I think that many of the problems that we face as intelligence officers we've got to deal with . . . ourselves and accept the reality that the policy world is out there, and we have to interact with

There was general agreement that the idea of a red line is somewhat artificial, especially in the new circumstances since 9/11.

I think that intelligence officers too easily want to blame the policymaker for their problems.

it . . . . We've got to solve many of our own problems, and they have nothing whatsoever to do with red lines or with the policy process.

* * *

But the idea that intelligence can ignore the political atmosphere in which it's being delivered is, again, a Panglossian affliction.

* * *

We were not the least bit reticent in saying, "You go this way, you're going to have a wreck." But it wasn't a case we were saying the policy was good or bad. That was supposed to come from somewhere else. And I think it's not a matter of a red line; it's just that there were different jobs.

* * *

From the discussion, I get the impression that the failures of the intelligence side and the failures on the policymaking side, and maybe some of their inability to communicate, are perhaps more serious than the transgressions of a red line, which is hard for us to define at the present time.

* * *

If we ever take away the transparency and competition, then that will be a lot more dangerous than any red line issue. I don't mean transparency giving away secrets; I mean everybody's opinion . . . any wacko wants to come in is fine as long as you've got to go up to the plate just like the rest of us.

* * *

You could say that, in administrations that tend to look at cooperation and hearing all views, the red line problem is real. In administrations that don't care to hear all views and [tend] not

[to] listen to a different set of approaches and attitudes, it isn't the red line problem that's most important.

* * *

In President Clinton's administration, there was an effort to reach out and coordinate and make sure everybody's views were heard, [to reach out] to the academic community to make sure that competing views and assessments were brought into the equation as [the] decisionmaking process was moving on . . . . there was a concerted effort at that kind of consensus building.

* * *

The other problem that we have . . . is the problem of the Intelligence Community being coopted by the policy community and that distorting the process to the point that it yields counterproductive results. And perhaps here the . . . answer is a more sophisticated understanding on the part of the Congress and the American people of how these institutions operate and what their limitations are and the recognition that the Intelligence Community will occasionally be coopted by the policy community, as a result of which its findings and conclusions will be less reliable and simply accept that as a consequence of the necessity of the two to interrelate on a fairly intense basis.

* * *

In the end, the person you elect as president is going to have to determine a lot of this. And, like a lot of other things in this country, there's no organization chart. There may be a set of rules in the Constitution and elsewhere, but I don't think there's an easy way to say, "Here's the red line. Thou shalt not cross."

* * *

First Speaker: *That red line is certainly not a bright one, and it might not even, who knows, it may not even be red. You know, it kind of may be some other shade.*

Second Speaker: *Yellow or amber.*

Third Speaker: *Probably gray.*

Voice from the audience: *Probably gray, right.*

* * *

If we were still living in the world of September 10, I think there would have been quite a spirited debate on the nature of the red line, where the red line is today. But, as we found out quickly in the afternoon, in many ways, we've moved beyond that. And it may come back to the fundamental issue that we're at war.

Key Questions

What do policymakers want from intelligence? Consider the full spectrum covering raw intelligence/finished intelligence including analysis/multiple policy options and implications/policy advice/policy advocacy?

What factors determine the extent to which policymakers expect a greater/lesser role for intelligence in the policy process? For example, is the expectation dependent on whether the policy issue concerns a denied area (closed society or no regular diplomatic contact)? How about issues that involve extensive covert action (Afghanistan)?

How do policymakers deal with unwanted policy advice from the Intelligence Community? Ignore it? Set up a separate intelligence shop? Stop inviting intelligence officers to policy deliberations? What happens when intelligence officers refuse to give policy advice?

How do senior intelligence officers see their role along the spectrum from information provider to adviser to advocate in policy formulation and implementation?

How does this role change when covert action transforms the DCI into a force provider/commander?

What criteria should govern future decisions on crossing the red line between intelligence and policy? Is there now or should there even be a red line when homeland security is involved?

Should a new "red line" be established? Where should it be? Should intelligence officers assume a primary role for formulating policy? Should they make policy suggestions? Should there be a distinction between the two?

How does a policy role for intelligence officers affect their objectivity?

www.ingramcontent.com/pod-product-compliance
Lightning Source LLC
Chambersburg PA
CBHW080402290526

45790CB00009BA/3665